BRUTAL COMPANION

Ruben Quesada

Cover Art: Ruben Quesada
Cover Design: Catherine Charbonneau
Interior Design: Michelle Caraccia

Published 2024 by Barrow Street, Inc.
(501) (c) (3) corporation. All contributions are tax deductible.
Distributed by:
Barrow Street Books
c/o University of Rhode Island
English Department, Swan 114
60 Upper College Road
Kingston, RI 02881

Barrow Street Books are also distributed by Itasca Books Distribution &
Fulfillment, 210 Edge Place, Minneapolis MN, 55418, itascabooks.com.
Telephone (844) 488-4477; amazon.com; Ingram Periodicals Inc., 1240
Heil Quaker Blvd, PO Box 7000, La Vergne, TN 37086-700 (615) 213-
3574; and Armadillo & Co., 7310 S. La Cienega Blvd, Inglewood, CA
90302, (310) 693-6061.

Special thanks to the University of Rhode Island English Department
and especially the PhD Program in English, 60 Upper College Road,
Swan 114, Kingston, RI 02881, (401) 874-5931, which provides valuable
in-kind support, including graduate and undergraduate interns.

First Edition

Library of Congress Control Number: 2024943575

ISBN: 978-1-962131-03-2

BRUTAL COMPANION

Ruben Quesada

Barrow Street Press
New York City

CONTENTS

I

II

III

ACKNOWLEDGEMENTS

I

Blessed are those who mourn, for they will be comforted.
— Matthew 5:4

TERMINOLOGY

My mother is going to die. Her ashes
will be sewn into the ocean, stitched

onto passing angelfish. I think of what
she'll look like when she dies, as if

permanently sleeping, slivers of lids
closing her off from me. Like a torrent

swelling against the curvature of bone
embracing my lungs, my breath fails

to escape the natural order of things:
dawn, dusk, unequivocal heartbreak.

Her silhouette flashes and I think
of you next to me every morning.

It'll be years from now, but you, too,
will appear to be asleep when I discover

you, as if cast from porcelain or
copper like Hermes waiting

at a museum in Rome; from dust,
from a fragment of rib, your nearly

opened lips weaving breath in
the tongue of light, your smooth

figure at my side—and I will know
then, Aristophanes was right

about two halves of man faring
through life in search of each other.

ACATALEPTIC

In time you, too, will find yourself—
in fleeting moments, in the next stanza, in the next

monosyllabic word: *thin*, its airy hum vibrating
in your nose. I am in these lines you are reading.

We are here with these words, like a moving object,
whose echoes fill our ears like a sonic boom.

AFTER HOURS

I wander for miles. Overhead, a skyscraper looms street
    after street.
I turn the corner into an alley to find warmth.
    Like Morse code, bloodshot semaphores blink
    overhead—

            redrum, redrum.
A gust pushes me onto the curb,
    delivering concrete, sanding my hands and knees.
        Last night at a loft in downtown L.A.
        I took too much MDMA.
Here, behind dumpsters where the light is grey from smog,
and cobwebs comb the undersides of another day.

        Hours past midnight,
    only the streak-throated swallows
   perched on power lines
like sixteenth notes are safe.
    Into clouds cracking with a peal of lighting, they go.

ON PROGRESS

Beyond the amplitude of sky filling the pulverized windows,
a plane plummets toward us. We evaporate into a cloud
uttering cries that rise with an explosive shift
of wind, like dust. Above these desks,
pendant lighting pivots like the cacophonous cracking
of a whip. The roof hurries to hush walls closing
down upon us; see the swelling floor tiles
swallow the room; we are weightless,
falling into each other, stuck like bandages
holding wounded steel and flame.

A.I., or ARDOR'S INCANDESCENCE

Christ suffers in reverent gold on crucifixes, gifts
from the elderly, all over the walls. ~~Omar~~ embraced
his role as hospice lead.

His office harbored a hide,
stretched and dried, a tan sling darker than bronze,
with steel studs and rings, a hue he yearned to summon
every summer.

We smoked, listened to Helen Reddy's melody,
then Grace Slick urged us to feed our heads. We consume clouds
numbing our mouths. A caterpillar calls and she sings, as you lie
on my chest, supple and sleek.
An incoming windstorm rattles our embrace
like live wires. Your eyes widen, I slip my feet
into stirrups, my legs raised high
making a steeple of myself.

THE RESURRECTION

After Piero

Moments earlier the moonlight undressed the air. You've returned to this mortal coil dressed in an ascending tremolo of light. Your hallowed face hemmed by blood; to your right a sleeping providence of trees, to your left the waking decay of leaves curbing the falsetto plea of loss. And the counterpoint of starlight swoons through the blood of soldiers at your aspiring feet.

PYRE OF A VANISHING PLANET

Highways slow and begin to bow to a raging fury
    from a torrent like a lion's roaring on a distant coast
        as a breeze steals our breath away
    and the sky lights up in bloodied bloom
we cannot ignore. Charcoal lids sizzle, brownstones beaten
    as smooth as suede whirl with grace. Petticoat palms aglow
    like beacons stipple each boulevard. Along Sixth Street's viaduct
    looking for consolation in the night on an arch that spans horizons
and connects East and West, we choke, cough it out and
        bless our breath. We are tired of this savagery. But who will
    rescue us from this alien sway as bodies entwine in a nuclear ballet.

AFTERLIFE

I am Orpheus drifting in the night,
like a cataract light begins to flicker.

The light does not diminish. I am
diminishing in the dark.

A cataract is a beast of a flicker, a veil
of apparent magnitude from interstellar dust.

I must continue to seek
the one I must.

Keep moving!
Do not descend.

In time you will adjust.

FERVENT THROATS

We left a window open
and the waking sky filled
its wide, beechen mouth.

Beneath me, your chest full
of curls in the unseen grooves
of your clavicle. Full of spring

starlings begin to gather
among the leaves and we listen
to music filling their fervent throats.

AND REVERIE

          An arrow toward the sun—
lines of geese blackened like grease
against the sailcloth of sky. In time some die,
while others fly away in a balmy burst
and soon more will return to fulfill
their pursuit of small tremors of love.

IN LUBBOCK, TEXAS

There's a park with dips
and mounds of crabgrass
streaming into patches
of rust-colored dirt
where you ride
your horse. It's always hot

in Texas. Even in winter,
the snow doesn't stay
for more than a night
or two. Nothing ever
wants to stay in Lubbock.

I mean, no one ever
wants to be there—
with its mediocre produce
and vacant walkways,
worn and cracked. Nobody

bothers to walk anymore.
That's what pick-up trucks are for.
You drive two minutes
to the store and back. There

is a song that says,
happiness is Lubbock
in the rearview
mirror. Bless, Mac Davis!

Bless, Buddy Holly! Here
in the dark, the branches
brush against the glass
always watching from above.

Still, I have no idea what
a horse is like. Of course,
of course, I've seen them
on television as a child.

I watched *The Lone Ranger*
and *Mr. Ed*. For a time, I believed
animals could talk. I have
never known a horse but

I've always talked to my pets.
My snow-colored parakeet
named Frosty sang to me
when I spoke to him, I mimicked

learning to conjure the spirit
of his music in my mouth. But how
does one speak horse? I've read
that a horse's ear is as delicate as

the skin of a girl's wrist. Their buttonhole-
dark eyes are a storm that never
settles, looking into you as it breaks
the Earth with only a whisper.

MOONLIGHT

After George Inness

I cannot bear to close my eyes
because I don't want to see the end
of this night. Come! Come and draw

your loose lines of light against and
into my open mouth like the fine lines
of a web being built along my heavy face,

lead-bellied, blood-clotted clouds of night's
sleep borne brooding of your bright breast
keeping me from rest while you lie

upon my chest—the weight of your body
spread, your coarse beard presses
into my neck. Give me leave. Leave me

like this night of my marriage to the moon's
urgent flight. Leave me outright for day's light.

ON PRESENCE

For René Magritte

Will you   see the faces you once heard about
from your neighbor's eight-year-old son   days before

he died,   as you look out toward the sky? Those apple-faced
angels watching   through the drawn curtains of the window

where the rain has streaked your view   into tobacco-
colored sunlight smoking   the bedroom; onto the bed

where you awoke last night to find the fabric of space   wrinkled
like the bridge   above your nose; remember the disproportionate

weight of dark matter heavy on your bottom lip   the balm of
your body against my mouth

YEAR OF THE DRAGON

I stayed up all night
The first time at sixteen
After snorting amphetamines
Down the street from home
In Hollywood with a man
Who I'd visit when
I wanted to get high
Cigarette after cigarette
To talk about books
Before and after
Chasing the dragon
Until the sun rose
Then I'd leave
He'd go to work
I'd walk home
How we first met
I can't quite recall
Like the drugs
He was always on call
The lights spun
My legs in the air
I can't remember a time
When I didn't give in
The drugs and the night
Our foiled animal skin

OATH OF THE HORATII

After Jacques-Louis David

In memory of their final departure
fill the discontent, unlit rooms beyond

the background with the prescient splendor
of youthful rejoicing; let the budding waves

of a child's cry cut into you like the serrated
edges of angels' wings—move past the inevitable.

God is dead; surrender to the eager eyes of murder,
turn away from the nascent light and hurl yourselves

onto the ground, twisted like the wilted stem
of an anemone. Pray in the shadowed crossing

of their swords for these soldiers to return alive; if
the children could speak they, too, would take the oath

and follow. Oh, if only I could fathom the dizziness
of your grief; your wretched frames spinning in silk robes.

SLC PUNK!

The last time we parted, I looked past you as snow banked
along the curb. Patches of sidewalk glowing brightly, and a wide
hunk of clouds hovered above like the unfinished background
of a painting. In the distance your unbuttoned smile, your blue jeans

stirring an electric storm with its yellow seams sizzling down
your thighs. Last night as we lay in bed, we talked about one-night
stands we'd had. You told me about the time in Salt Lake City
where you spent a night in a sling, high on heroin, and a line

of married men waiting their turn to be inside you. The smell
of the fireplace filling your nose is what you remember most.
Beyond the window, mountains blanched with snow. You slowly
fade behind a sugar maple, branches like scarecrows waving goodbye.

THE HAUNTING OF UPTOWN, CHICAGO

I

I've started to see shadows,
  and they've become more frequent—
tall and thin, with long faces.

    The sun is far from rising. Storefronts
     are still decorated for Halloween.

    I hurry down the street,
     my head down against the wind.

    Is someone standing outside of your window?

Across the street, a shadow begins
  to follow me on the way to the train station.

II

The wisdom of owls
  ignore everything. Constellations unfold above.
     I push past turnstiles
     on time to board.
         The morning fog is thick
         and heavy, like wet wool.
         The train passes
         Graceland Cemetery.
I can't tell if this is real. I haven't slept
in two days. My weekend
  has started to overstay its welcome.

III

At the next stop, a bearded man
  in a white shirt and black tie enters.
He sits and holds a Bible in his lap.
    At the next stop he moves
      to the door. I am facing him.
    He undoes his tie. Streetlights turn
the hair on his chest and skin the color of amber.
    He tugs at his pocket and I watch
        his erection settle to one side. A wet spot
          forms at the base of his zipper. He looks up
at me and doesn't break his stare. Looking out
    above the Chicago River, the train jerks
and I turn away, not recognizing myself
        in the reflection, I laugh splitting the silence.

ON AGING

Jazz was not only built in the minds of the great ones,
but on the backs of the ordinary ones.
—Cab Calloway

Forget the obscure optimism
of the Atomic Age that subdued us
with supersonic flights, ascending
skyscrapers, and horsehead pump jacks. Recall
instead the energizing glamour of the Jazz
Age sheltered among the heady speakeasy
breath of Hennessy, the Eighteenth Amendment,
and radio broadcasts. Now, our digital heart
slows to analog speed and in two hundred
years you, too, will forget the vision
of Manhattan masked by fire and smoke;
its skyline like a steam locomotive migrating
toward the sea—a fog of fumes, ghost and
ash, blackened roofs of America—chugging
toward Liberty Island. Remember the towering
lights mirrored on your lips, the oxidized
epithelium of your lungs seizing the air.

ANECDOTE OF AN AIRCRASH

I dreamt
I was

        a weightless ribbon
        an astronaut
alight
in a lilac hurricane

        of sunlight
        on the first morning
        of flight
I am alone

        in the warring morning
with a lit cigarette
I flick it   off a bridge

        when my flesh gives in
above a lagoon of lights
past traffic
past freeway

        do not enter
into the past
I stare   and watch
cars everywhere

        stuck together
all over town
I am
in love

        with rows of planets
        and comets
coming   into view
toward a queue

        of clouds

I am drunk
on this highway
                    we loved
                    a boom of smog
                    meets me
a tensile curve of the road
                    a forest of homes rise
                    with lilies
I'm tired   of being told
the world won't be
                    worth much
in a million years
                    though it can't be true
                    or must never be
how difficult
it must be   in this body
believe me   in this flesh
watch   this car fly
                    in the distance
cargo ships sail
                    we fly
well past   tomorrow
                    like a god
through the night
                    thick with stars

HOUSE FIRE

Work was brief, as usual.
I've been sitting on a bus in traffic
on Lakeshore Drive for over an hour.
To the right, Navy Pier booms and whistles
above the black milk of Lake Michigan.

In 1871, meteor debris fueled Chicago
into flames. Lake Point Tower shimmers past
Navy Pier like a wounded sea sapphire.
My body is at its limit.

Fall approaches as the Earth passes
through comet debris left by Hailey's Comet
in 1986; I watched it from the window.
The radio reports comets coming,

I am nine late on a Sunday. Next door,
the family returns from church to find
their six-year-old, his room aflame, melting
the curtains above their kitchen sink.

II

You want me to tell you the marvels of invention?
That we persevere.

— D.A. Powell

LIEBESTOD

Dear listener, you've come to expect this version
of a love story: the drizzle of love's fog descends
to wreck families, leaving two lovers collapsed
into each other's arms. You'd hoped it would end
another way, maybe this time events would contravene
the conventional but, after centuries, the unraveling
of tradition even in a story leads to death. And yet
the imagination awakens within like the petals
of moon flowers opening to evening's effulgence;
intuition sways you to seek the final embrace of dissidence.

GENESIS

Even the province of truth must be stitched; start
with a pattern, a needle and thread, to sew the empty
sleeves of a sentence—a hole in the hull of a hemistich.
We'll begin by weaving a heroic couplet with the tip
of our tongues then spit and spin fringe for flare. Thread
a loose sentence. Darn it. The slip stitch of subject
and predicate through ribbed velveteen. Then
set tender baroque buttons on the cuff and press
an adverbial crest over the breast. What is the point
predicated on subject and verb. The smell of your bronzed
skin in my mouth—a periodic splinter on the road
of my spine along the wall. The collar curls
a path to trace the past as the hem unravels.

WE HUSBAND

Our own history   like the measure   of particulars

    is rarely exact;   we are a shade   or a fragment

    of dust   neither created   nor   destroyed: a range

    of light whose chemical properties are seen

and   unseen. To appease   our guilt   we   calculate

   the mystery   of our making; imagine   waking

in another   age   where the compass of conception

    is revealed   only moments   before we end

   up like the Pillars   of Creation   whose

   extinction   hasn't yet presented itself   to us.

AUBADE

Antelucan, we lie—your body moons against mine. Earlier,
I stoked sweat on your neck in the humming of this light.
In the dark, I listen, now resigned, you mumble
about the arms of pinyon pine, saying it points to a falling star
against the serrated pool of sky. We hear the grackles chatter
as they fly past a church lot. Then headlights shine on your face
splitting your face, listless lips, half-open eyes—staring out
I wait for the occult wreckage of night to vanish from this world
and hold out until its final moment until I fall asleep
and get lost. Your body is light like tulle carried off
by a strong current—taken from me—as I helix in the light.

ON WARFARE

Now, I am become Death, the destroyer of worlds.
                                        —Vishnu

To understand an atomic bomb
   you must remember
      nuclear fission creates free photons
and neutrons when its magnetism is broken.
   Like a meteor or an angel crashing down
      whose heaviness rains its patient radiation
in waves, almost nothing survives its sibylline glow.
   The blossoming ionization of wind will fill lungs—
      few people will laugh, few will cry, most will be silent.

COUNTRY WORDS

For America

A word unheard
to hullabaloo
cubchoo, I slurred
namby pamby too

aloud in a crowd
combing my hair
in a honeycomb
house & a pair

approach the door
confer a barbed cry
not heard before
in this jungled sky

queer fandangled words
blanket the air
amid upswept rooms
caribou herds

gutting white-haired
moss chew gummit loose
a four-flush scared
juicy calaboose

rice truck quirley pross
roostered Western glow
brassy Betsy Ross
spangles in tow.

AFTER THE FLOOD

When the song says, Even the sun sets
in paradise, I think of you and my body breaks

into mists—dear friend—who once laughed
and wept. Sitting in the next room I heard you;

the slow note of your exhale as you slept
like an oboe's mumble fogging the air.

It still lingers. I never imagined
the body's music could charm me.

And why should any song
have a purpose. Don't go

toward the light. The light
in you eclipses your sorrow—

you are a garden
in the sky.

ON COMMUNION

A purple wing crushed upon the windshield

        impels me to ask if there is a heaven

                for this creature

delivered on the bald tires of a decaying machine,

            its joints worn from years of prayers

              fading into exhaust,

leaving tarnished streaks washed by rain in its wake.

    Past the stained glass

        you see the semblance

      of a resurrected cloud forming overhead; maybe

            it's in the shadows that embody

        the shape of a familiar form;

your view is refracted by the abundance

    of rain—it's hard to believe a road lies ahead.

BILLOW OF THISTLES

Yokeless on a dimly lit coast
oxen settle along the shore
only to be concerned with themselves.

In Ireland, my man left
and joined a Jesuit order.
I went and met a priest
—I must confess. He said,
Come with me.
Come and smell
the stone roses.
Taste the sweet coral
honeysuckle sap
of Earth. What's best
on windy days
Antilles lilies
wash over us.

Donkeys trot along a caramel,
sunlit marsh beyond
the amplitude
of my outstretched legs.
Above us, Christ sags
on the cross. In a billow
of thistles, seaside olive trees
cleave in a field, whipped
by the wind, they ripple
like the loose neck of a goose.

Waves of light spin
into Adam's body, as if
Eve appears from silk.

WITH A LINE BY PAUL MONETTE

On the night we met, I smoked
a pack of Camels on the porch
with you. Many summers ago,
we drank iced tea by the pool,
swam beneath a tantrum of cicadas.

Today, while you were at work, I learned
another way to leave you. I did laundry,
took a Xanax, and folded a syringe
and tourniquet into a drawer.

PYTHIAN APOLLO

After Leochares

In the curved mouth of your breast
where your heart once roused the alabaster
of your gaze, now forever
rediscovered; the elastic energy
of your twittering arrows await
their spiral release from your abrasive hands;
the rising arch of your foot moving
forward to shatter the myth
of your aspiring aim that slays
serpents and gods alike. If the seraphic drape
of your almighty shoulders could sing,
its hymn would speak the dour tales
of your passion—you'd be unrecognizable,
eclipsed behind a bearded wreath of blood.

ON KNOWING

Nothing brings a lover back
from the dead. Listen. When I pray
I hear the rabid-belled horn release
its bark against the outstretched
bodies of violins who already know
our cries do not belong among them—
the instrument of my voice propelled
like a frayed cloth that holds the wretched
stain of grief; perhaps the merciful voice
of the flute that cuts in upon a harp
wooing a tuba and tenor trombone
will remain loyal long after silence gnaws
at our throats. God, forgive me if I find
no fixed design in the downfall of man.

COMPOSITION

For Raphael

Christ is supported by two angels
two copies of you; their faces clouds

of light oxidized over time; a cirrus
fibratus of faces delivered into life in grave

shadows seized by smudges of lead. Hands hold
Christ's elbows as if they'd raise his plunging body

with their faith, his blood runs down his forearm
into the cup of their hands. The saints must have

guided your soiled fingers through the ribbon
of his hair to frame the brilliant brow over

the eyes that dress his prostrate face
like constellations wearing the night.

ONE DAY

Consider the laborer,
waking, spending
      the crepuscular hours
      walking past freeway
entrances, against a flurry of traffic lights
to meet the clock, the anxious pedestals
      of loading docks. His shift assembling
      greased gaskets, tubes
drift by on a conveyor belt; a belt

that could ferry him home if it were built for feet. Home,
      where the eyes find the perennial astonishment
of morning. Consider how the sun sinks
      past the barrage of asteroids that initiate a quip
on the electromagnetic stipulations of the day.

DECOMPOSITION

In this blood that haunts my skin, in the folds of my brain are burrowed the harrowed words to describe you—bleak, cursed. And when the universe was young, it possessed the means to give you breath, to deliver you here, for me. On this last day, you'd stumbled, half alive, onto the drawn curtain in the corner of your room. We watched ghostly orbs of light one last time drifting in like laughter. An ice cream truck's siren song shook you back to life from the hunger for heroin. Outside, children passed. Photographs browned like honey from years of smoke covering the walls. I watched you from your bed where so many worlds undressed beneath the sap-like weight of phosphorous. Could the periodic table offer much more? Already, you were sulfur, even gold.

AT THIS TIME OF YEAR

I board the express train while summer simmers
in patches of rain. The subway car rails into a turn
as the sun needles at my neck. We dive down
into a tunnel buried deep like the dead.

I watch an owl forego the tunnel's threshold toward
a streetlight; its body bulges in the amber
gleam and its wings appear to split.

At home, as I sit at my desk, the clock dings for a sixth
and final time. I take a rosary of metal up to my lips
like a clarinet as the quick rhythm of the second-
hand clicks. From next door, the jacarandas
have started pushing against the window.

ON WITNESS

For Paul Monette

Dear Stranger,
Look out.
Flattened clouds
fill the horizon.
They please
the flat-earthers.

Grey bodies
at the windows
gloss as you lose
your smile
reflected
in winter's
glen as
the temperature
rises.

Let's
say you've
become
the sky.

Let's say
your face
is full
of dawn
drawn
in the glass
as the car
begins
to weep.

HERETIC or THE PLAGUE

Like that visit to Roswell we
        took. As it slept, a fire began,
                and the sky circumvolved
like streams coiling around.
        We were storms at peak then.
                        I want to rewrite the algorithm
of our time together. We've never understood the problem.
        Refine my logic, you said.

This is not a test. When lightning strikes
                the windows crack to reinvent themselves
                with the speed of a whip.

ANGELS OF PARADISE

After Marc Chagall

Come with me.

Let me show you
the blue field
of light that soothes
aching feet.

Lie on waves
of lavender
growing beneath
your feet—this is paradise.

Your tongue tastes
air scented
with pumpkin
and rosemary.

Roses, rosebud
budding, bend
and smell—lingers like sap—
the magic of daylight
will warm you
and cover you
in its golden embrace
—a marsh-marigold
folding into you.
You're covered
in a glaze.

Gaze
into my eyes,
children, gaze
into the honey
colored creatures—
it is time
to find a place
of rest—soon
the dark
will come
and shake you
into the orchard
of undress.

WOMAN IN BLACK

After Édouard Manet

I am no longer
in control—
you and I will
soon discover
we take pills
to find each
other. In this
ghostly hour
we fall into this
queer half-sleep.

At first, I cry
out, just a peep.
Watch me unfurl
like a lizard
on a bough,
then I appear
at your feet
in a cloud.

You move
toward
swaying
like an oak
with arms

outstretched,
sunken, your
face begins
to sing—
your voice
grows
like a slit
of moonlight
amid the trees.

Your lips
peel like
blackened
lace, and I
take a pill
to forget.

ON MOUNTAINS

Enchanted monolith, the horizon rests
            upon the highest cuestas
of your veined brow. To the North
            against the butte
solar mist reaches for us like a golden
            hand; branches fan
the spine of a stream. It doesn't seem
            possible an entire planet
hovers in a flurry of gravity.

THIS IS THE WAY THE WORLD ENDS

A body at rest is the color of a new moon,
a hue so dim you begin to imagine
your own body glows in the pitch of night.

Before bed, peel the scabrous coat off
your face, flesh pressed and gone to the bone,
dried out like jerky on the bathroom floor.

Nothing survives without water. This is
the will of the body. This cannot be undone.
Moments later, a bang was heard,

few were awake when it happened.
A deafening whistle rattled the brain—
the world went mute. This cannot be undone.

Then came a heat—the world's heat rose
to meet the body's blood boil. This is
the will of the body. The body—splits

into atoms, faces yawn into skulls.
We sun. We become.
We become undone.

OATH KEEPER

Dawn unwinds over coppiced topped tree-lined
sidewalks, pushing its way into tunnels
and alleys. After hours on my knees,
I abide by an oath of secrecy.
A voice says your throat feels as soft as silk.
Last night began with a fury of men—
otters and well-hung wolves—muscular, packed
against the window of a rented room.
They don't stop until frost pierces the shade
and my raw, anchored breath clouds around us.

SHADOWS

I stand on our lawn
when a girl passes
swiftly like a shadow
I watch her wait
at the corner crosswalk
as birds dart into trees
my eyes blur
a car begins to slip
across the horizon
her body flails
toward the curb
my mother appears
in the crowd
we stand tightly tucked
it's Mary in a dress
the color of asphalt
she is the color
of skim milk
months later
Mary's mother
is found
in the garage
with the car running
before we
attend her funeral
the radio announces
Rock Hudson is dead
for him there was
no funeral
only a body
the color of ash

CONNOISSEURS

For Marianne Moore

Certain sunsets are purple lights kissing
snow-covered rooftops. Or taking a sheet
of paper to compose a love letter
in purple-colored ink—but I have seen something
more desirable, a simple image
of a child's wrist. Or far better, moving
pictures of the world I inhabit—

I am transported to a parallel
universe I have sought all my life. We
stand in the street as a car idles and
moths crowd into the light. It is late. Steam
from our mouths conjures smoke signals; night feels
colder than it is. In a few days, snowfall is likely.
The air fills with the smell
of birch. Mirrors enlighten and delight.
Humans are wondrous. Poets are wondrous.
This I like best.

THE POET

For Picasso

It was winter. The night was blue, the streets
framed by piles of snow. Barefoot, to avoid
waking the rest of your household, you led
me back to your room. I held you firmly,
our chests swelling against each other. Your
cheek yielded to my shoulder; the sleek strung
canvas of your back cooled in my arms, nape
cradled in my hand like the slender neck
of a guitar. You whispered in my ear:
What is there in life except one's ideas,
good air, good friend, what is there in life?
Friend, there is the product of this moment
we share—ideas we hold and this affair.

A PAEAN

Take me. Take this.

My wasted life
and all
its bliss—the sea
of your body
with its warm
grip on night's
wrist. Your lips
curled into me.
Your eyes
set me loose
in a foggy
lake. Loons
call to fill my
deadened heart.

To know what loss
is like, you must
lose everything,
you must lose
even yourself,
you said.
I am alone.

Each night I lie
and learn
to sing
the dead back.

You are the bloodied
cracks in my skin
so deep; I keep my
hands together
to hold you in.

Hear me. Here this.

III

We can never be with loss too long.
— Spencer Reece

ON VOICE

For Carl Sandburg

An evening escape from the butchery
        of Union Stock Yards; wife and daughter
camp along the tracks of Leavitt
        Street—the manifold skyline blooms
into a constellation of skyscrapers; beyond
        the veined traffic lights,
two nameless, fiery stones huddle in a corner.
        What of the seraphim in flight above
this brilliant Earth wrapped in the hale
        song of fecund wind? How could we know
what you know, how the blanched roads
        blackened boughs each winter, how the wild
lights of passing trains rouse your rural thoughts.

EAST OF WYOMING, I REMEMBER MATTHEW SHEPARD

After "The Entombment" by Raphael

The night my father died, I sat on a stool
    at the Buckhorn, gazing
        out the window's cool counter seat.
Like a funhouse mirror, you appeared.
    I have a familiar-looking face; my father used to say—
        his wish for me to blend in.
Late after an argument, I fled
    and was found bound to a prairie fence
        after eighteen hours.
My body is like a sock in the wind
    in a field just a mile from here.
        My face blooms, velvety
and light like a lamb's ear,
    stachys byzantina; my ears
        frozen with blood; down
my neck, it goes. A medley of ants shuffles
    away. My body is rich with the sour smell
        of urine on my head like a crown of daffodils.

I WAS A BOY

As a boy, I was unbearably uncomfortable
about my body and the men my mother dated
gave me erections in the bathroom
as I thought of them under the hiss
of the shower to drown out the catcalls
from boys at school who threatened to kill me

every afternoon. I have tried to avoid
blaming myself for being called a faggot
for most of my life, I could not escape it
but those days have gone like the gospel
of Anita Bryant, who wanted to drown

a faggot rebellion like Stonewall
in the summer of 1969. Once, I was a man
who curated mediocrity like the time
I misspelled peniaphobia to conceal
my fear of having spent my life
penniless, undressing only in the dark.

FOR ICARUS

After Brueghel

Oh bankrupt youth, time has come
   to take the gleaming hand of mortality—
      awaken to the volatile elements around
         you. Fugitive, flung from the sky, yield
            to the trapdoor of light leaving a constellation
of feathers sweeping the sea; you have
   scarcely a breath to cry out, the lungs
      suffering with the rise and swell of waves
         rippling past the canticle of kelp. The magic
            of your wings dissolved, the sun serenely
turns away delighted by its sovereignty. Oh
   gods, asleep in things around us, how clear
      it must appear, now in receding red tide,
         that faith has always been fleeing from us.

WATCHING DANIEL V. JONES

The tallest interchange ramp in Los Angeles
is at the intersection of the 105 and
the 110, where the alchemy of orange and
red traffic flows beneath sunsets like
wildfire. Once, a man named Daniel V. Jones
drove to the top of this ramp after a car chase
and parked. It was late in the afternoon,
an interruption of after-school cartoons,
as news broadcasts announced his name.
He had cancer. His insurance failed
to provide healthcare to save him. Jones,
with his hair and clothes on fire, exited his truck,
took a shotgun to his head as the windshield blew out.

ANEW

We've the elegance of hoary grass,
the magnolia's grace, the stamina

of ocean and sky; we sprout like sunflowers

into air, our lungs branching
like wild oaks or the deepening fissures within

glaciers. Forgive the slug and the snail

for their patient attack—they too must eat.
The radiation of life is constant, and we all must

submit to its silent, unseen influence. We grow

old because we are old, as the sunflower
that grows old because it too must die.

There was time before and time after.

LIVE BROADCAST

At sunup, he positioned you in front
of a mirror and moved in from behind,
banging his body into you. Life is a series
of addictions. Years later, you'll find him
online to relive that moment when you
gave your life away like R. Budd
Dwyer did in 1985. A flurry of cameras
off-screen screams as he says, this will hurt
someone. A group of reporters spills out
of the room. He holds a revolver. His hand
rises like a copperhead colt until it rattles
like the Holy Spirit out of his head.

THE CROWNING

Lord, you who
have never left me like a fading shadow at day's end.
You settle,
a silent stone
in the sweet
arteries of my hand: golden crocus forming
your forgotten body.
How
it must feel
to let go,
to be free,
to be me.
In praise of you
let me sing this once,
a shimmer of your light, a crown of fire
dying in the night.

ANGELS IN THE SUN

After JMW Turner

Few imagined being bound to this world—
extraordinary, ordinary—they rose, a crucifix
flying into the ruddy gallows of heaven.

Stunned by their flashing lights aflame
across the bow of their spacecraft—landing
lights for that world. Herds of animals:

horses, humans, and fish fixed.
The angels approached.
Come, angels! Come beasts!

Men and women cried out to each other—
the angels cried—some were lost
between their earthly life and paradise.

I would have waited alone
a thousand years for the coming of angels
to abandon this world for another.

ON BEING

Everything looks like a Monet
painting, the details softening
onto the curve of road;
the reddened trees slicing
through crumbling clouds
of smog. The moon gives itself
up to engorged highways
glowing through the windshield.
A bewildered driver waits
at a stoplight— who has turned
this image around? Now I'm a thin
column curiously looking past
the farthest queue of cars.
The light changes, the driver
grows smaller moving past,
I am a ribbon of flesh
waving in the mirror.

MY MOTHER IS A GARDEN

She plants razzleberry fringe flowers in the backyard
as the chartreuse golden feather fare well next door.
Before my birth, she is acquired by the United States—
coerced by the American zodiac dream, she fled to Los Angeles—
decades later, she still withholds from speaking English and
only fertile names of flowers have taken root. She is luminous.
Her hair, a blackish grey against the philodendron, parted
long. I lose her in the shade of overgrown impatiens hanging
onto the hillside behind the house. The horizon undulates with
barberry and nettles, deer grass waves of silver. Years have passed,
not speaking with my mother, but today, I surprise her with a visit.
In the glow of the window, I watch her tend to her roses and
notice that I have taken the shape of her hips.

THE FORTUNE TELLER

Christ
nevermore
than a man
nailed
to a cross
but
from him
I learned
a life
can fit
into a palm
like a book
of poems
I learned
confession
won't save me

I'm reminded
of a fortune
teller I met
in San Francisco
at Dolores Park
on a radiant
late
afternoon
as the sun
slanted
across
bodies
of slackline
wrapped
palm trees

From the shade
came
a woman
wearing
a green scarf

She hooked
herself
into my arm
took me
toward her

She took
my other hand
made it float
face-up
into the pool
of air
between us

She fingered
my palm
into creases
of sevens
or Ls

She sketched
a future
I once
wanted
into neat
curves

from thumb
to wrist

Then
my hand
dropped
and her scarf
drifted
into the trees

She coughed

The barrels
of her lungs
wheezing
—exhausted

She turned
away, wiping
her mouth
and said
last night
as your
mother
died,
a haze
of zinnias
hushed
in the rain

ACKNOWLEDGMENTS

Thank you to everyone who helped to launch this book into the world. Especially, the extraordinary editors at Barrow Street Press: Rachel Rothenberg, Shannon Carson, and Peter Covino; and my publicists, Zoe-Aline Howard and Cassie Mannes Murray. Everyone for your care and vision to make this journey possible.

Thank you to all my teachers, friends, and community for nurturing me and my work over the years. I continue to learn from you. To the readers who offered me their support, in advance of this publication: Jericho Brown, Paul Hlava Ceballos, Laurie Ann Guerrero, and Spencer Reece.

Special thanks to Bryan Borland and Seth Pennington and their team for publishing many of these poems in a chapbook as *Revelations* (Sibling Rivalry Press 2018).

Grateful acknowledgement to the following publications and anthologies for publishing these poems, in some iteration: *Academy of American Poets, The Adroit Journal, The American Poetry Review, The Believer, Berfrois, Cimarron Review, Cordite Poetry (AU), Honey Literary, Kweli Journal, Mumber, The New York Times Magazine, North American Review, Pilgrimage, Pleiades, The Poetry Foundation, Quiddity, The Rumpus, Seneca Review, Southern Humanities Review, Spoon River Poetry Review, Superstition Review, Taos Journal of Poetry, TriQuarterly, Tupelo Quarterly, The Best American Poetry 2018*, ed. Dana Gioia; *Essential Queer Voices of U.S. Poetry*, ed. Christopher Nelson; *Leaning Toward Light*, ed. Tess Taylor; *Between Paradise and Earth*, eds. Nomi Stone & Luke Hankins; *Alone Together*, ed. Jennifer Haupt; and *A Night of Screams*, ed. Richard Z. Santos.

This collection of poems was developed in a variety of artistic and scholarly communities across the country. I am incredibly grateful to the institutions that provided space, time, and support for my research and writing. These include fellowships at the Virginia Center for the Creative Arts, Jentel Foundation, and Santa Fe Art Institute; transformative conferences and workshops like the Napa Valley Writers Conference, Lambda Literary, Vermont Studio Center, Community of Writers, and Tin House; and critical cultural organizations like the AWP Latinx Writers Caucus, CantoMundo, Letras Latinas, and the Smithsonian National Museum of the American Latino.

My academic journey, which helped shape this work, included time at UC Riverside's MFA program, Texas Tech University, Antioch University, Cedar Crest College, Columbia College Chicago, UCLA Extension, and Mercy Street, as well as local Chicago institutions such as the Dollhouse, Chicago Review of Books, NewCity Lit, and the Chicago Literary Hall of Fame, all had a significant impact on me. I am deeply grateful to all of these organizations and the individuals within them who have helped me grow as a poet and mentor.

I have had privilege to meet many of you who have welcomed me into your communities and spaces in-person and online. Sometimes I resisted asking for help, and sometimes I asked for too much. To all of you, I send my love and gratitude, if I have not mentioned you here—for believing in me, for your friendship, and much more.

With special gratitude to Ada Limón, Adam O. Davis, Alex Espinoza, Alison C. Wellford, Amanda Moore, Amy Danzer, Ananda Lima, Andrea Change, Andrew Wells, Anna Leahy, Anthony Cody, Ariel Francisco, Aricka Foreman, Benjamin Garcia, Brenda Cárdenas, Brian Spears, C. Dale Young, C.T. Salazar, Camille Dungy, Carlos Cumpián, Carmen Giménez, Carrie Muehle, Casey Plett, Cecilia Weddell, Charlie Jensen, Chloe Garcia Roberts, Chloe Honum, Chris Campanioni, Christopher Buckley, CM Burroughs, Claudia Rankine, Connie

Voisine, Cristina García, D.A. Powell, Dan O'Brien, Daniel Lassell, Daniel Olivas, Darren C. Demaree, David Biespiel, David Campos, David Groff, David Tomas Martinez, Deborah Ager, Diana Pando, Diego Báez, Edward Kelsey Moore, Éireann Lorsung, Elizabeth Burke-Daine, Elizabeth Metzger-Sampson, Elizabeth Taylor, Emily Pérez, Adrian Ernesto Cepeda, Faylita Hicks, féi hernandez, Frederick Speers, Gary Jackson, Gerry LaFemina, Greg Edmondson, Gregg Shapiro, Grisel Y. Acosta, Gustavo Hernandez, Holly Amos, Ian MacKinnon, Ignatius Valentine Aloysius, ire'ne lara silva, J. Mauricio Espinoza, Jacob Saenz, Jacob Shores-Argüello, Jan Beatty, Jay Besemer, Jeannie Ludlow, Jean-Pierre Rueda, Jeff Walt, Jen Benka, Jennifer Harris, Jen Karmin, Jeremy Lybarger, Jesse Fleming, Jessica Guzman, Jim Sullivan, JJ Hernandez, Joanne Diaz, Jory Mickelson, Jose B. Gonzalez, Joshua Young, Juan Felipe Herrera, Juan Morales, Julia Borcherts, Julianna Baggott, Kai Coggin, Katie Manning, Keetje Kuipers, Kelli Russell Agodon, Kenji Liu, Kenyatta Rogers, Kevin McLellan, Kimberly Ann Southwick, Kirsten Reach, Kyle Behen, Kyle Churney, Larry O. Dean, Lauren Cerand, Lawrence Kaplan, Leah Umansky, Leslie McGrath, Leticia Hernández-Linares, Lisa Hase-Jackson, Liz O'Connell-Thompson, Luis Alberto Urrea, Margaret MacInnis, Mary Hawley, Mark Rennie, Mary Kim-Arnold, Maureen Seaton, Maurya Simon, Melinda Palacio, Michael Dowdy, Michael Montlack, Michael Slosek, Mike Puican, Millicent Borges Accardi, Miranda Weiss, Nadxi Nieto, Nan Cohen, Natanya Pulley, Nickole Brown, Nicole Sealey, Nik De Dominic, Noah Fields, Norma E. Cantú, Paisley Rekdal, Paul J. Willis, Rebecca Gayle Howell, Rebecca Hazelton, Richard Scott, Richard Siken, Rita Banerjee, Roberto Harrison, Roger King, Rosa Alcalá, Roxane Gay, Sandra Beasley, Sarah Rae, Sasha Hemon, Sergio Troncoso, Shane Khosropour, Stephanie Barbé Hammer, Steve Bellin-Oka, Steve Young, Stuart Barnes, Sue Landers, Sydney Lea, Taylor Brorby, Tim Miller, Tom Lutz, Tomás Q. Morín, Toni Nealie, Trevor Ketner, Tyler Allen Penny, Valerie Martinez, Vickie Vértiz, Victoria Chang, Vicki Hudson, Vincent Toro,

Viva Padilla, and Ydalmi Noriega.

For my family: Charley Wasson, Virginia Vargas, Jorge Vargas, Kathy Quesada, Gabby Quesada, Ken, Frank, Mitchell, Niccole, Mathew, Tatiana, Brianna, Thalia, Theodore, and Nathaniel; Theresa & Jerry Christmas, Anne Gallagher, Dan & Bill Kuzcek, Robert Markley, Stuart Keeshin, Cruz.

Billy, my love.

Ruben Quesada is the editor of the award-winning anthology *Latinx Poetics: Essays on the Art of Poetry*. His poetry and criticism appear in *The New York Times Magazine, Best American Poetry, Lambda Literary Review, Harvard Review* and elsewhere. His collection of poetry, *Brutal Companion*, is the winner of the Barrow Street Editors Prize.

BARROW STREET POETRY